OCS Study
MMS 2001-078

Coastal Marine Institute

How Does Produced Water Cause a Reduction in the Genetic Diversity of Harpacticoid Copepods?

Final Report

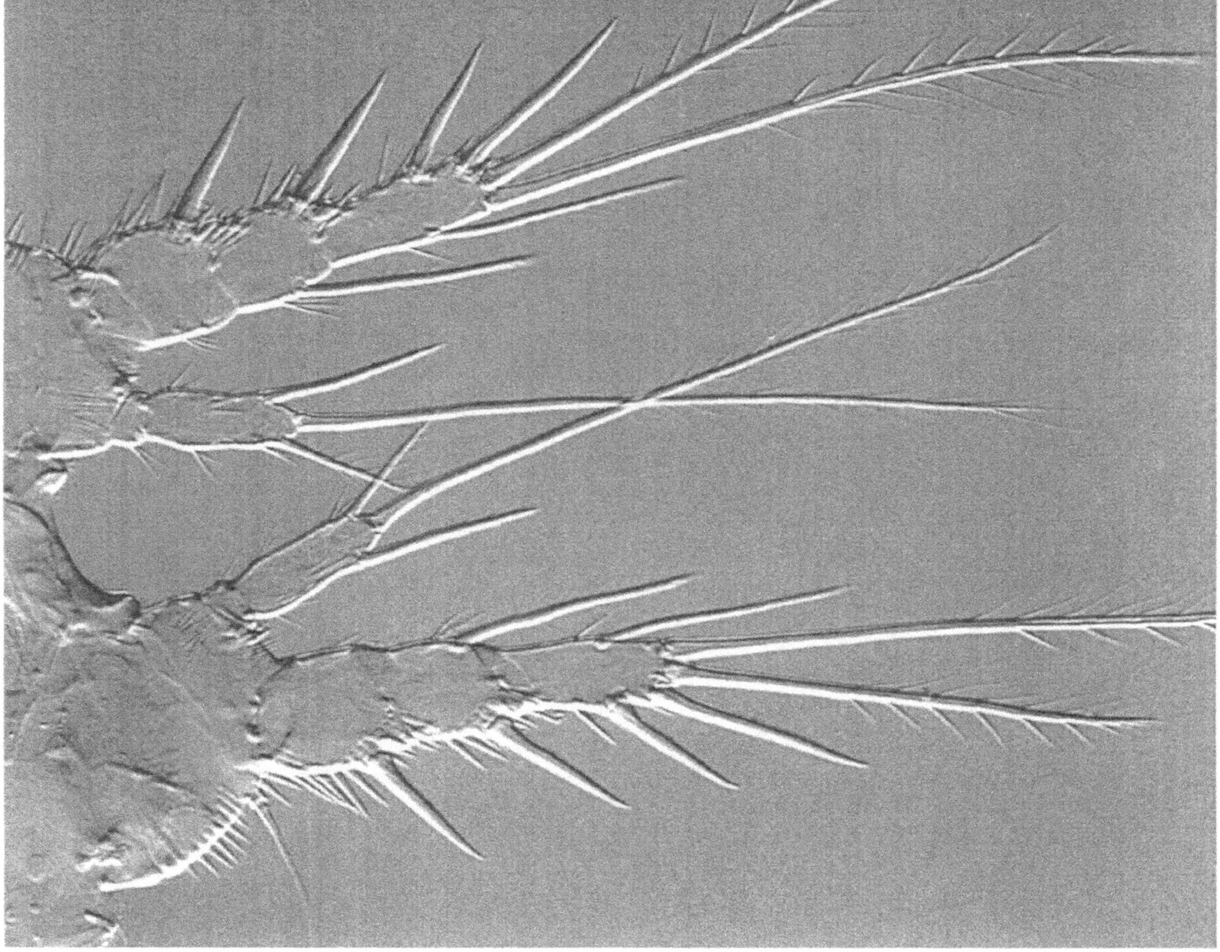

 **U.S. Department of the Interior**
Minerals Management Service
Gulf of Mexico OCS Region

 Cooperative Agreement
Coastal Marine Institute
Louisiana State University

OCS Study
MMS 2001-078

Coastal Marine Institute

How Does Produced Water Cause a Reduction in the Genetic Diversity of Harpacticoid Copepods?

Final Report

Authors

John W. Fleeger
David W. Foltz
Axayácatl Rocha-Olivares

September 2001

Prepared under MMS Contract
14-35-0001-30660-19949
by
Coastal Studies Institute
Louisiana State University
Baton Rouge, Louisiana 70801

Published by

U.S. Department of the Interior
Minerals Management Service
Gulf of Mexico OCS Region

Cooperative Agreement
Coastal Marine Institute
Louisiana State University

DISCLAIMER

REPORT AVAILABILITY

Extra copies of the report may be obtained from the Public Information Office (Mail Stop 5034) at the following address:

U.S. Department of the Interior
Minerals Management Service
Gulf of Mexico OCS Region
Public Information Office (MS 5034)
1201 Elmwood Park Boulevard
New Orleans, LA 70123-2394

Telephone Number: (504) 736-2519 or
1-800-200-GULF

CITATION

Suggested citation:

Fleeger, J.W., D.W. Foltz, and A. Rocha-Olivares. 2001. How does produced water cause a reduction in the genetic diversity of harpacticoid copepods? Final report. OCS Study MMS 2001-078. U.S. Dept. of the Interior, Minerals Management Service, Gulf of Mexico OCS Region, New Orleans, Louisiana. x + 35 pp.

ACKNOWLEDGMENT

We thank John McCall, Markus Wetzel, Debra Dexter, Samuel Gómez, Ana Puello-Cruz, Mark Ohman and Annie Townsend for specimen collection or donation and Mary Martin, Deb Taranik, and Nannette Crochet for laboratory assistance.

ABOUT THE COVER

The third swimming leg of a specimen of *Cletocamptus deitersi* (genotyped as type II) collected near Port Fourchon, LA.

TABLE OF CONTENTS

LIST OF FIGURES

LIST OF TABLES

1. ABSTRACT

Cryptic species (morphologically-similar but genetically-distinct sibling species) may contribute to observed reductions in genetic diversity at contaminated sites (a) if some taxa among the groups studied form a cryptic-species complex in which cryptic species co-occur at uncontaminated sites, and (b) if cryptic species exhibit different responses to contaminants such that differential mortality among cryptic species occurs at contaminated sites. We studied the common and wide-spread harpacticoid copepod *Cletocamptus deitersi* to determine if it is comprised of morphologically-similar species and if these cryptic species are sympatric. We also conducted toxicity bioassays with *C. deitersi* from two locations with both poly-nuclear aromatic hydrocarbon and metal contamination. Our molecular and limited morphological analyses suggest that at least four putative species of *C. deitersi* are found in North America and that two of these co-occur at two intensively-sampled locations. Furthermore, these molecular types display different toxic responses to heavy metals, suggesting different tolerances at contaminated sites. These data suggest losses of genetic diversity at contaminated sites may be associated with losses in species diversity due to a reduction in the number of cryptic species caused by contamination. Future studies using genetic diversity as a marker of contaminant effects should consider the possibility that cryptic species may contribute to losses in genetic diversity.

2. How Does Produced Water Cause a Reduction in the Genetic Diversity of Harpacticoid Copepods?

2.1 Introduction

Oil and gas exploration and production activities in the marine environment produce and release large quantities of organic, hydrophobic compounds and heavy metals. Unfortunately, the effects of these toxicants and their causal linkages with benthic and pelagic biota are difficult to identify and are frequently poorly understood. Research associated with the GOOMEX project (Kennicutt et al., 1996; Peterson et al., 1996) identified an intriguing phenomenon: a loss of genetic diversity in meiobenthic copepods was found in close proximity to production platforms (Street and Montagna, 1996). The magnitude of this genetic change appears to be consistent with contamination gradients, and is equal to or greater than the response seen with several traditional indicators (e.g., body burdens, biomarker activation, community structure and toxicity) based on species- and community-level attributes. Specifically, Street and Montagna (1996) analyzed the16S rRNA gene of the mitochondrial genome in several meiobenthic harpacticoid copepod species by polymerase chain reaction (PCR) and restriction fragment length polymorphism (RFLP) analysis. They found a reduction in genotypic (haplotype) diversity in harpacticoid species collected in close proximity to production platforms.

More generally, the effects of contaminants on genetic variation in marine organisms have been studied for about two decades (reviewed by Hebert and Luiker, 1996). Previous studies of genetically-controlled protein variation (reviewed by Hummel and Patarnello, 1994) have produced inconsistent and even contradictory results in that exposure to contaminants (heavy metals have been most frequently studied) has led to increases and decreases in genetic diversity compared to unexposed populations. Genetic adaptation to contaminants may occur quickly under strong selective pressures imposed by moderate to high levels of contamination (Brown, 1976; Klerks and Weis, 1987; Klerks and Levinton, 1989a, 1989b; Klerks, 1990; Mulvey and Diamond, 1991; Posthuma and Van Straalen, 1993) and lead to increased tolerance of contaminants. Thus, the relationship between genetic structure and contaminants is likely to be complex, and cause and effect may be difficult to assign.

A loss of genetic diversity associated with studies such as Street and Montagna (1996) may have several causes. A reduction in genetic diversity may be the direct result of exposure to contamination via the process of genotypic selection. Selection may favor some genotypes/haplotypes over others causing genetic change. Sediment contamination is not a likely cause of selection for or against the rRNA gene used by Street and Montagna (1996) because its function is unrelated to any known detoxification mechanism. Linkage with other genes in the mitochondrial genome that may be under selection is presumably responsible for the loss in diversity of rRNA genotypes (the mitochondrial genome is completely non-recombining) if selection is the cause. Linked gene effects are not limited to the mitochondrial genome, and are potentially important for understanding the effects of contaminants on nuclear-encoded proteins (Gillespie and Guttman, 1993). Heavy metals and poly-nuclear aromatic hydrocarbons (PAH) are elevated in close proximity to production platforms, and either or both could provide the selective pressure necessary to reduce genetic diversity. Analysis of sediments along

3

distance gradients around the GOOMEX platforms suggests, however, that heavy metals are more likely to occur at concentrations that may cause mortality or chronic reductions in reproduction than are PAH (Peterson *et al.*, 1996). In addition, a population that is reduced in abundance by exposure to a contaminant may experience a population bottleneck. If so, genetic diversity may be lost through the process of genetic drift. Street *et al.* (1998) conducted a laboratory selection experiment on *Nitocra lacustris*, an estuarine harpacticoid copepod. They found that under strong selection from phenanthrene (a compound frequently used as a model PAH), loss of genetic diversity of the 16S rRNA gene occurred. They concluded that the observed reduction was not associated with resulting small population size, and their work suggests that selection may cause the reduction in genetic diversity associated with Street and Montagna's observation. Therefore genetic diversity has been proposed as a new marker for contaminant effects.

Alternatively, it is possible that some of the mitochondrial DNA genotypes found in the GOOMEX study represent interspecific variation in the form of cryptic species rather than within- species variants. Cryptic species are morphologically-similar but genetically-distinct sibling species. Such complexes are known to occur within numerous cosmopolitan and previously well-studied (based on classical morphologically-based systematics) marine invertebrate taxa (Knowlton, 1993). Furthermore, Warwick and Clarke (1995) point out that many colonizing species frequently found in polluted habitats are actually complexes of cryptic species. Although the possible existence of cryptic species has been mentioned in some previous studies of pollution effects (*e.g.*, Pearson and Rosenberg, 1978), few investigators have explicitly examined this possibility. Cryptic species have been found to occur in widely-studied pollution indicator species (*e.g.*, Grassle and Grassle, 1976; Lobel *et al.*, 1990), and in harpacticoids (Bergmans, 1979; Battaglia, 1982; Ganz and Burton, 1995) and other meiofaunal taxa (Todaro *et al.*, 1996). If cryptic species with differing levels of pollution tolerance occur among harpacticoids, the apparent reduction in genetic diversity near platforms could represent a loss of species diversity rather than genotypic selection. The frequency with which cryptic species complexes are being discovered with molecular techniques suggests that this explanation is possible, and that caution should be applied in future work that utilizes genetic diversity as a marker for contaminant effects.

Meiobenthic harpacticoids are small crustaceans that range from about 0.4 - 1.5 mm in length and average about 1-3 μg in dry body mass as adults. This small size may inhibit the detection of cryptic species (Costello *et al.*, 1996). Harpacticoid taxonomy is based on morphological characters that must be visualized with high-power microscopy after whole-body dissection. Furthermore, closely-related species that require dissection for identification may be sympatric among harpacticoids (Gee, 1988). The advent of sophisticated optics (*e.g.*, differential interference microscopy) now allows the use of detailed observation of body ornamentation and traditional features important to crustacean taxonomy such as mouthpart structure that has produced extremely rigorous taxonomic criteria (Huys *et al.*, 1996). Modern taxonomic standards suggest that apparent cryptic species can be resolved morphologically (Lee and Huys, 1999), and many cryptic species are likely to become pseudo-cryptic species complexes. However the dissection required for detailed morphological observation destroys tissue, precluding DNA extraction and intense taxonomic analysis on the same individuals. Thus,

4

individuals for which DNA extraction is to be conducted can only be examined cursorily at low magnification; cryptic or closely-related pseudo-cryptic species may be missed. Large numbers of specimens (over 300 per species) were processed for genetic analysis by Street and Montagna (1996), increasing the chance of encounters with rare species and thus the chance that mis-identifications. If species mis-identifications are common, resulting estimates of genetic diversity will be inflated. If species diversity is reduced near contaminated areas, an apparent reduction in genotypic diversity will result. Studies using RFLP may be especially prone to this criticism, because restriction enzyme digestion samples only a portion of the nucleotide site diversity present in a particular gene region and may underestimate the true amount of divergence between sequences (DeGiorgi *et al.*, 1990). Also, sequence data allow comparison to a large body of previous studies on molecular divergence of invertebrate taxa at widely-varying taxonomic levels for numerous mitochondrial genes. For these reasons, in the present research project we used direct sequencing of PCR products as our primary molecular technique.

A key question regarding species complexes has to do with tolerances to contaminants. If cryptic species have different tolerances, then a community exposed to this contaminant may selectively lose species in contaminated areas. Previous work has suggested that cryptic species have unique tolerances to contaminants (Hogg *et al.*, 1998; Sturmbauer *et al.*, 1999; Linke-Gamenick *et al.*, 2000), but no similar study has been conducted with harpacticoids, although (Kovatch *et al.*, 2000) reports that intra-specific variation in tolerance to contaminants exists.

Cletocamptus deitersi (Richard 1897) is a canthocamptid meiobenthic copepod with a highly cosmopolitan distribution reported from inland brines (seeps, streams, and lakes), as well as coastal estuaries and mangroves in all continents except Europe (Mielke 2000). This species has been shown to be morphologically polymorphic within and between populations (e.g., Fleeger 1980; Mielke 2000). For example, Fleeger (1980) reported consistent variation in setal patterns of the third and fourth swimming legs among specimens from a single location; these differences could not be discerned without dissections. *C. deitersi* is similar to many harpacticoids in that it lacks a planktonic dispersing larval stage (free-living larval stages develop in sediments), and adults and juveniles are capable of short-distance (meter-scale) dispersal through the water column (Sun and Fleeger 1994). This species is unusually tolerant of salinity variation (Simpson *et al.*, 1998; Dexter, 1995) and has been found to be highly resistant to hydrocarbon contaminants (Carman *et al.*, 1997) and disturbance (DeLaune *et al.*, 1984). The geographical isolation of inland brines suggests that long-distance migration and colonization events are rare and that gene flow should be limited among inland populations. Morphological variability and potential for geographic differentiation make *C. deitersi* a good candidate for analyses of geographic genetic variation aimed at determining the existence of cryptic (or pseudo-cryptic) species.

Using a multilocus genetic approach and limited morphological observations, we analyzed *Cletocamptus deitersi* from four localities in North America to determine if separate populations are represented by morphologically and/or genetically differentiated species. Two sites were intensively sampled to determine if cryptic species live in sympatry. We also obtained genetic data from *C. helobius*, a readily identifiable and morphologically differentiated congeneric species, to establish a reference level of indisputably interspecific genetic differentiation. An undescribed harpacticoid (Canuellidae: *Coullana* sp.) and a planktonic calanoid (*Calanus pacificus* Brodsky 1948) were used as outgroups in copepod phylogenetic reconstructions. In addition, tests for tolerance to PAH and metal exposure were conducted on *C. deitersi* from two locations.

2.2 Materials and Methods

Copepod samples and DNA extraction

Samples were collected at an inland brine seep near Jackson, Alabama (June 1998, 31°23'N 87°53'W) and at two locations on the coast of Louisiana (Port Fourchon, December 1998, 29°05.4' 90°05.8'W and Cocodrie, January 1999, 29°15.2'N, 90°39.8'W). *Cletocamptus deitersi* was also obtained from laboratory cultures established from collections made in the Salton Sea, California (July 1997, 33°13'N 115°52'W), and at the mouth of the "Estero del Yugo" estuary (January 2000, 23°18.14'N 106°29'W), in Mazatlán, Sinaloa, Mexico. These environments are very different. For example, salinity at the Alabama brine seep reaches 45‰ close to the source, and the stream is located in a bottomland forest subject to annual flood and drought cycles, some 83 km from the coast. The Louisiana salt marsh is tidally flooded and salinity ranges from 0-28 ‰. The Salton Sea, where salinity has recently increased to > 45 ‰, was created in 1905 and is more than 100 km inland from the Pacific Ocean and from the Colorado River Delta in the upper Gulf of California.

Field-collected copepods were removed from sieved sediment and fixed in 95% ethanol. All harpacticoids were carefully identified by one of us (J.W.F.). We extracted total genomic DNA from individual copepods based on Schizas *et al.* (1997). Ethanol-preserved specimens of *Calanus pacificus* from southern California (32°25'N 119°58'W) were provided and identified by Annie Townsend (Scripps Institution of Oceanography). DNA extraction for these copepods was done by standard proteinase-K digestion and phenol-chloroform-isoamyl organic extractions, followed by ethanol precipitation.

PCR amplification and sequencing

All copepods were subject to an initial PCR amplification of the mitochondrial DNA (mtDNA) cytochrome oxidase subunit I (COX-I) gene using universal primers (Folmer et al. 1994, 0.72 mM total dNTP, 2.5 mM $MgCl_2$, 1 unit of Promega Taq in manufacturer's "A" buffer; Perkin Elmer 480 thermal cycling was 10min at 95°C, followed by 40 cycles of 15s 95°C; 30s 40°C; 60s 72°C, and a final extension time of 5min at 72°C). We sequenced two additional gene regions in copepods representative of the major lineages identified on the basis of COX-I sequences (except for the Mexican copepods for which all gene regions were sequenced in all individuals): (1) part of the mitochondrial large subunit ribosomal DNA (LSU rDNA 16S), amplified using Palumbi's (1996) 16SAR and 16SBR universal primers, and (2) part of the nuclear rDNA, comprising the entire ITS1, ITS2 and the intervening 5.8S rDNA, amplified using Heath's (1995) ITS primers (cf. Table 1 in Heath *et al.* 1995). We designed *Cletocamptus*-specific internal primers for re-amplification of weak initial reactions (COX-I: CLEintF TTTTGATTTTCTYATCCAGC and CLEintR CCTAGTAANGARGAAATTCC), for

6

amplification when universal primers failed (16S: 16SciF YTAAGGTAGCATAGTAA and 16SciR TTAATTCAACATCGANGTC), and for sequencing of long PCR products (nuclear rDNA: 5.8SciF GGGGTCGATGAAGAACG and 5.8SciR CCCTGAGCCAGACATGG). Target PCR products were electrophoresed, excised from gels (2% agarose), purified using columns (QiaQuick, Promega), and sequenced using Applied BioSystems ABI-Prism Big-Dye terminator chemistry (Perkin-Elmer) in scaled-down reactions and run on an ABI-377 Gene Analyzer. Representative nucleotide sequences have been submitted to GenBank (AF315001-AF315033).

Multiplex haplotype-specific PCR

We designed a rapid, cost-effective method of large-scale genotype screening of individual copepods, using a multiplex haplotype-specific PCR reaction (MHS-PCR, Rocha-Olivares 1998), to assign copepods to one of the first two COX-I mtDNA major lineages. Initial LCOI–HCOI amplicons were used as template of the MHS-PCR, in which the size of the products, visualized in an agarose gel, could be used for PCR-based genotyping. Multiplexing with nested primers produced a positive control amplicon in all haplotypes and a second haplotype-specific amplicon, whose size would be diagnostic (Fig. 2.1). All MHS-PCR batches included experimental positive and negative controls. We sequenced a number of copepods genotyped with MHS-PCR to verify the accuracy of the method.

Data analyses

Orthologous nucleotide sequences were aligned with the Clustal W algorithm (Thompson *et al.* 1994) with default parameters. In mitochondrial and nuclear rDNAs, inferred indels were further adjusted by eye to minimize those separated by one or very few bases. Aligned nucleotide sequences, with the exception of ITS regions, were used to reconstruct gene trees using maximum parsimony (MP) and neighbor-joining (NJ) with the program PAUP* 4.0b4a (Swofford 1998). NJ searches were made with distances computed using a best-fit model of nucleotide substitution. Models were fit to each data set (COX-I, 16S, and 5.8S) under a maximum likelihood framework and tested for significance (overall $\alpha = 0.05$ after Bonferoni correction) with likelihood ratio tests (LRT) using the program Modeltest 3.04 (Posada and Crandall 1998). Branch support was assessed by 1000 non-parametric bootstrap replicates. Phylogenetic analyses of the mtDNA 16S rDNA were performed on the data set bounded by 16SciF-R primers (313 base pairs [bp]), not the entire 16SAR–BR alignment (466 bp) that was incomplete for the Mexican *C. deitersi* and *C. helobius*. Competing phylogenetic hypotheses and the existence of a molecular clock were tested under a likelihood framework with LRTs. The program Seq-Gen (Rambaut and Grassly 1997) was used for parametric bootstrapping of datasets. Rates of synonymous and non-synonymous susbstitutions were computed following Yang and Nielsen (1998) with the program PAML 3.0b (Yang 1997).

Morphological-genetic comparisons

The number of inner setae on the distal segment of the third swimming-leg exopod of both sexes is known to differ within and among *C. deitersi* populations (Fleeger 1980) and in related species (Mielke 2000). To determine if morphological and genetic patterns correlate in

C. deitersi, 51 specimens from Louisiana and 23 from Alabama were examined morphologically and genetically. The third leg was removed with a fine probe, mounted on a microscope slide, and examined with phase microscopy. The remaining copepod tissue was used for DNA extraction and genotyping by MHS-PCR. Specimens were given an identification number upon dissection, and genetic analysis was conducted without knowledge of their origin. In addition, the third leg exopod of several specimens from California and Mexico was examined and compared to specimens from the Gulf of Mexico.

Toxicity Tests

Phenanthrene and metal toxicity tests were conducted on *C. deitersi* collected from Port Fourchon, LA and from the Jackson, AL brine seep from November, 1999 - April, 2000. Copepods at both sites were collected by skimming the upper 1 cm of surficial sediments by hand. Collected sediments were placed in buckets and water from the collection site was added. Buckets were transported to Baton Rouge where the overlying water was replaced with 25‰ artificial seawater, and the green alga *Selanastrum capricornicutum* was added as a food source. After a five-day acclimation period at room temperature, copepods were removed from the sediment surface and overlying water by aspiration and sorted under a dissection microscope to be available for bioassays. Bioassays measured acute toxicity. *C. deitersi* was exposed to contaminants by aqueous exposure in 20 ml of 25‰ artificial seawater in 35X50 mm crystallizing dishes without food. During the experiments, copepods were maintained in a temperature-controlled incubator (at 25° C) in constant darkness. Bioassays with phenanthrene were conducted in triplicate with 10 *C. deitersi* per dish under saturated conditions (about 1200 μg phenanthrene/l) in 1 g/l acetone. The number of living *C. deitersi* after 96 h were tallied. Metal toxicity was tested with a mixture of three metals based on proportions representative of produced water (Zn 100: Pb 10: Cd 0.5). After a range finding test, 20 *C. deitersi* per dish were exposed to a solution of 6249 μg Zn/l, 685 μg Pb/l and 62 μg Cd/l (verified by ICAP). The number of living *C. deitersi* in eight replicate dishes (and two control dishes) were tallied every three h for 96 h. Dead copepods from both experiments were placed in 95% ethanol and later genotyped using the multiplex haplotype-specific PCR reaction to assign individuals to a COX-I mtDNA major lineage. *C. deitersi* survivorship measured in toxicity tests after 96 h in each lineage was analyzed by pooling all replicates and utilizing goodness of fit tests. These tests include the z test and Fisher's Exact Test and were used to examine differences in survivorship frequencies between control and exposed populations and between type I and type II copepods (expected frequencies were equality). Sigma Stat software was used. Finally, the Cox-Mantel test was used to compare survivorship curves generated by types I and II individuals exposed to metals using Statistica software.

2.3 Results

Genotypic variability

A total of 135 copepods (121 *Cletocamptus deitersi*, 7 *C. helobius*, 2 *Coullana* sp., and 5 *Calanus pacificus*) was initially sequenced for one or more gene regions. The number of distinct COX-I haplotypes per locality ranged from one (Mazatlán) to 10 (Alabama) (Table 2.1). COX-I sequences fell in one of three major types, which will be hitherto referred to as "major types" or "major lineages". Type I was found among copepods from Alabama, type II predominantly among organisms from Louisiana but also in Alabama, whereas type III was exclusively present in all copepods from California (IIIC) and Mazatlán (IIIM). A small fraction of copepods from Louisiana also harbored type I sequences.

Of all the *C.deitersi* genotyped of types I and II (sequencing + MHS-PCR, total N = 240), 11 (7.7%) from Louisiana harbored type I and 132 (92.3%) type II COX-I sequences. Conversely, 90 (92.8%) *C. deitersi* from Alabama had type I whereas only seven (7.2%) had type II. All COX-I sequences obtained from 15 haphazardly selected copepods genotyped via MHS-PCR (both type I and type II) corroborated the identifications obtained with the PCR-based method. Eleven distinct 16S sequences were found among 47 *C. deitersi* analyzed (Table 2.1). Overall the 16S rDNA followed the same pattern as the COX-I, in that sequences fell in major types analogous to those identified earlier.

We obtained nuclear rDNA sequences from 23 *Cletocamptus deitersi*, four *C. helobius* and one *Calanus pacificus* (Table 2.1). The nuclear gene regions showed different levels of variation, ITS being the highest and 5.8S the lowest. Except for the Mexican copepods that shared two distinct ITS1 alleles but only one ITS2, the rest of copepods had the same number of ITS1 and ITS2 distinct alleles. In sharp contrast, the 5.8S rDNA showed very low variability with only 4 distinct alleles among the 23 *C. deitersi* and two among the four *C. helobius* (Table 2.1). However, no nuclear alleles were shared between the two congeneric species. In both ITS regions, alleles assorted into three extremely divergent groups, each matching the major mitochondrial types (I, II, and III) previously identified on the basis of the mtDNA sequences. On the other hand, one of the four 5.8S alleles was shared by individuals with different mtDNA types, notwithstanding the fact that in each organism the same 5.8S allele was flanked by drastically different ITS alleles falling in the divergent groups described above.

Intra- and interspecific levels of genetic differentiation

Levels of genetic differentiation within each major type of *C. deitersi* were small and typical of those found among conspecific organisms, leading to the assumption that each type represents a putative species. Mitochondrial genes were less variable (0.2% to 1.7%, diagonal of Table 2.2) than non-coding nuclear ITS regions (2.7 – 8.5% in faster-evolving ITS1 and 0.7 – 2.6% in ITS2, Table 2.3). As expected, intra-lineage variation in the slowly-evolving 5.8S rRNA gene was virtually absent. Although copepods from Mazatlán are unequivocally most closely related to those from California, they are quite differentiated in both mitochondrial (11% in COX-I and 5% in 16S rRNA) and nuclear (12% ITS1 and 2.8% ITS2) genes (Table 2.3). Thus, four species may be represented within our three major lineages of *C. deitersi*.

Further evidence that our nominal *C. deitersi* is composed of more than one species comes from a comparison with its morphologically differentiable congener *C. helobius*. Organisms of the three major lineages of *C. deitersi* were as genetically differentiated from each other as they were from *C. helobius*. Corrected levels of mtDNA sequence divergence among the three major lineages were at least one if not two orders of magnitude higher than intra-lineage

9

divergences, values ranging from 48.7 to 88.3% (20.8 – 26.4% uncorrected) in the COX-I gene and from 29.4 to 82.5% (20.3 – 36.0% uncorrected) in the 16S rRNA (Table 2.2). The corresponding values of indisputably interspecific (i.e. *C. deitersi* vs. *C. helobius*) differentiation were 71.9 – 91.7% (23.7–26.8% uncorrected) for the COX-I gene and 63.1 – 81.4% (31.7–35.8% uncorrected) for the 16S rRNA (Table 2.2). Data from nuclear genes were consistent with mitochondrial results. In the case of the widely divergent non-coding ITS regions, nucleotide sequences of alleles from different lineages are so different that their alignment is dubious (Fig. 2.2). Conspicuous size differences (ITS1 lengths in each type were 359-376 in I, 292-300 bp in II, 288-289 in IIIC and 284 in IIIM; whereas ITS2 lengths were 221-228 in I, 204-206 in II, 215-219 in IIIC, and 216 in IIIM) and a large degree of sequence differentiation are indicative of a thorough randomization of the nucleotide sequences via mutation and recombination, such that statements of sequence homology can no longer be established confidently by alignment. Thus no quantitative appraisal of divergence is given (Table 2.3); instead, we present the imposed multiple alignment as qualitative evidence of the extent of differentiation (Fig. 2.2). The alignment shows that aside from the well conserved 18S and 5.8S rDNAs, the alignability of the sequences decays rapidly in the ITS regions but not to the same extent among the lineages of *Cletocamptus* since types II and III share more structural elements. Finally, in the slowly evolving 5.8S rRNA gene, mean levels of intraspecific variation in the nominal *C. deitersi* were smaller (0.6–1.5%) than the interspecific (3.7–4.6%).

Molecular evolution and phylogenetic analyses

The 16S amplicons in *C. deitersi* were either 462 bp (type I) or 467-468 bp (types II and III) in length. The amplified mitochondrial COX-I fragment was 658 bp long in all organisms. Almost a third of the nucleotides were variable (228 total variable sites, ratio of variable 1:2:3 codon positions was 43:8:177). Inferred COX-I amino acid sequences revealed that all nucleotide substitutions within types I and II were silent (details not shown). Most amino acid replacements were conservative with respect to hydrophobicity (20 out of 23). Rates of synonymous and non-synonymous substitutions along the lineages leading to types I, II, and III were $d_S = 11.19$ $d_N = 0.04$ (I), $d_S = 1.56$ $d_N = 0.006$ (II), and $d_S = 1.87$ $d_N = 0.007$ (III). Different models of nucleotide substitution were fit to each data set. For the COX-I gene, the best-fit model was Kimura 81 (Kimura 1981) with unequal base frequencies corrected for proportion of invariable sites (I) and for rate heterogeneity among sites (G) with a Gamma distribution (Yang 1993). For the 16S rRNA gene, the best-fit model was TIM (TIM+I+G Rodriguez et al. 1990); whereas for the 5.8S rRNA gene, the best-fit model was Jukes-Cantor (Jukes and Cantor 1969) (Table 2.4). The COX-I (Fig. 2.3) and 16S rDNA alignments including all taxa had, respectively, 309 and 215 variable sites (treating indels as missing data) of which 275 and 180 were parsimony-informative. The strict consensus tree of the eight COX-I most-parsimonious reconstructions obtained via branch-and-bound (length = 670 steps, CI = 0.72, RI = 0.91) was completely congruent with the NJ tree (Fig. 2.4). For the 16S, the NJ tree differed from the three branch-and-bound most-parsimonious trees (length = 419 steps, CI = 0.79, RI = 0.87) in that *Cletocamptus* was not monophyletic. Instead, *C. helobius* was sister to type I sequences and both were sister group to the rest of *C. deitersi* sequences (Fig. 2.4). A NJ tree constrained by monophyly of *C. deitersi* was not significantly different from the unconstrained tree (LRT, δ = 2.48, *p* = 0.43). In the MP analyses, the monophyly of *C. deitersi* had a non-parametric bootstrap branch support of 64%. Trees featured extensive unresolved polytomies within each major type (I, II, and IIIC) but were otherwise completely resolved. Both mtDNA gene-trees featured long branches, in excess of 30% corrected sequence divergence, separating the *C. deitersi* types I, II, and III, and the other congeneric and non-congeneric species. All bootstrap replicates recovered the monophyly of the three major mitochondrial types in both genes. Within type III sequences, the Californian haplotypes formed a reciprocally monophyletic assemblage relative to the Mexican with very high bootstrap support. Despite overall topological congruence of the gene trees, considering that a 16S NJ tree constrained by the monophyly of *C. deitersi* is not significantly worse than the one shown (Fig 2.4), the two mtDNA genes were not equally powerful in resolving the relationships of the major lineages within *Cletocamptus*. For example, the sister-taxon relationship between types II and III was very strongly supported by the NJ analysis of the 16S data set but less so by the corresponding MP analysis or by the COX-I data set (bootstrap 55 – 57%). Monophyly of *Cletocamptus* and Harpacticoida, however, was very well supported by the mtDNA data (bootstrap > 93%). The nuclear 5.8S rDNA alignment was 166 bp long with 32 variable sites, of which only 6 were parsimony-informative. An exhaustive search produced a single most parsimonious reconstruction (length = 33, CI = 1.0, RI = 1.0) and the NJ reconstruction was completely congruent (Fig. 2.5). Unlike the mitochondrial gene trees, the nuclear 5.8S rDNA proved more powerful for supporting the monophyly of *C. deitersi* (Fig. 2.5). Variation within *C. deitersi* was too small to gain any insight into the phylogenetic relationships among mitochondrial lineages. Branch-and-bound maximum likelihood analyses using best-fit models of substitution and one representative sequence of each *Cletocamptus* lineage, including *C. helobius*, indicated that the existence of a molecular clock could not be rejected in the mtDNA genes (COX-I: $\chi^2 = 2.89$, $p = 0.41$ and 16S: $\chi^2 = 6.04$, $p = 0.11$).

Morphological-genetic comparisons

All specimens of *C. deitersi* examined in this study had indistinguishable body plans (i.e., body length and width, rostrum shape, caudal rami shape and leg segmentation were essentially identical) and none could be distinguished by inspection with a dissection microscope and without examining dissected body parts such as swimming legs. Small variations in leg setation and body ornamentation have been described in species closely related to *C. deitersi*. For example, the number of inner setae on the distal segment of the third leg exopod of *C. axi* (one seta) differs from that of *C. schmidti* (two setae) in both sexes (Mielke 2000). Based on examination of the third leg exopod after dissection, all specimens from Louisiana, California and Mexico had one inner seta, whereas those from Alabama had two on the distal segment. MHS-PCR was successful in 70 of the 74 specimens in which the third leg was examined. Copepods with one inner seta on the third leg exopod distal segment, all from Louisiana, were of mtDNA COX-I major type II whereas those with two inner setae, all from Alabama, were of type I.

Toxicity Tests

C. deitersi has previously been shown to be very tolerant to PAH contamination (Carman et al., 1997), and our research with two major lineages suggests that both are highly tolerant to phenanthrene (Fig. 2.6). About 80% of type I and type II individuals survived exposure to

11

phenanthrene under saturated conditions for 96 h in aqueous solution. Goodness of fit tests demonstrated no difference in survivorship between exposed and unexposed individuals of both lineages (type I, z = 0.8 and p = 0.424 and type II, z = 0.716 and p = 0.474) and between type I and type II (Fisher's Exact Test, p = 0.759) individuals.

The two *C. deitersi* lineages tested were also both highly tolerant to metals; however, survivorship patterns differed among lineages (Figs. 2.7 and 2.8). Survivorship in both lineages to metal exposure was high until about 70 h. After 70 h, survivorship in type I individuals (all collected from the AL brine seep) decreased markedly to slightly less than 50% of the total while survivorship in the type II individuals (all collected from a LA salt marsh) remained above 75%. Goodness of fit tests suggested that survivorship after 96 h in type II copepods did not differ between metal exposed and unexposed individuals (z = 1.134, p = 0.257), while survivorship in metal exposed populations of lineage I was significantly decreased by metal exposure (z = 5.021, p < 0.001). Type I and type II survivorship differed after 96 h; fewer type I individuals survived (Fisher's Exact Test, p < 0.001). Furthermore, the Cox-Mantel demonstrated that survival pattern of type I and II lineages varied over time; the shape of the survivorship curves differed significantly (p < 0.001) (Fig. 2.8).

2.3 Discussion

For cryptic species to contribute to losses in genetic diversity associated with contaminated sites, three observations must be true. Firstly, some taxa among the groups studied must form a cryptic-species complex or be easily mis-identified (to act as cryptic species). One of the goals of this research project was to determine if a common harpacticoid copepod frequently found at contaminated sites is comprised of morphologically-similar species. The harpacticoid copepod *Cletocamptus deitersi* was selected for intensive study because it is known to be morphologically variable and highly cosmopolitan in distribution. In addition, *C. deitersi* in Louisiana consistently responds favorably to contamination by increasing in absolute and relative abundance compared to other harpacticoid copepods (Carman *et al.*, 1997). Secondly, cryptic species must co-occur at uncontaminated sites. Our research examined this possibility with *C. deitersi* at two locations. Thirdly, cryptic species must exhibit different responses to contaminants such that differential mortality occurs at contaminated sites. We examined this possibility by conducting toxicity bioassays with *C. deitersi* from two locations with both PAH and metal contamination. If these three conditions are met, it is possible that losses in genetic diversity at contaminated sites may be associated with losses in species diversity due to a reduction in the number of cryptic species at contaminated sites.

Our genetic analyses and limited morphological comparisons strongly suggest that *C. deitersi* in North America is not mono-specific (see Rocha-Olivares *et al.*, 2001 for a detailed discussion). Our analysis identified four putative species among specimens obtained from four widely-separated locations; additional collections may well yield more species. This conclusion is strongly supported by three lines of evidence. Firstly, molecular sequences revealed four extremely differentiated lineages with unalignable nuclear intergenic spacers and mitochondrial uncorrected divergences reaching 25% (cytochrome oxidase) and 36% (16S rDNA). These levels of divergence are greater than those reported previously for congeneric species in diverse

12

invertebrate taxa including crustaceans. Secondly, the intraspecific divergence among the lineages of *C. deitersi* equaled or exceeded the corresponding divergence from a known congener (*C. helobius*) with pronounced morphological divergence from the *C. deitersi* body plan. Finally, although all specimens of *C. deitersi* examined in this study had body plans (i.e., body length and width, rostrum shape, caudal rami shape and leg segmentation were essentially identical) that could not be distinguished at magnifications attainable with a dissection microscope, small differences in leg setation were detected between molecular lineages. Specimens from Louisiana, California and Mexico all had one inner seta on the distal segment of the third leg exopod, whereas those from Alabama had two at the same location. Furthermore, MHS-PCR was successful in genotyping 70 specimens in which setation from one leg was also examined. Copepods with one inner seta on the third leg exopod, all from Louisiana, were of mtDNA COX-I major type II whereas those with two inner setae, all from Alabama, were of type I. Even though leg setation could be environmentally determined (*e.g.*, by higher salinity at the brine stream), Fleeger (1980) found that both third-leg morphotypes co-occur in Louisiana, suggesting that leg setation is not a non-genetic response to environmental differences between coastal and brine-seep habitats. This suggests that setation is not an rapidly evolving, adaptive character under strong habitat-specific selection. Work in progress (Gomez *et al.*, unpublished) has identified differences in body ornamentation among all four putative species that are consistent with separate-species status using morphological criteria currently applied in harpacticoid taxonomy, and plans have been formulated to publish formal descriptions.

Based on our molecular data, two species within the nominal *C. deitersi* co-occurred at each of two intensively-studied field sites. Overall, 11 (7.7%) of the specimens we examined from Louisiana harbored type I and 132 (92.3%) type II COX-I sequences. Conversely, 90 (92.8%) *C. deitersi* from the Alabama brine seep were of type I whereas seven (7.2%) were of type II. Similarly Fleeger (1980) found two morphological patterns in a collection of *C. deitersi* from Louisiana corresponding to type I and type II designations, suggesting that co-existence of sympatric species may occur over long periods of time. If a study of genetic structure in *C. deitersi* using RFLP was conducted from either site and if a large number of individuals was processed for genetic analysis without examination of relevant morphological features (*e.g.* the third leg), both species would likely be included and coded as a single species.

To test how such a mis-identification would influence RFLP results with *C. deitersi*, restriction sites for 186 commercially-available restriction enzymes in the 460 bp region of the16S gene were inferred from the primary sequence data for type I and II *C. deitersi*. The number of restriction enzymes surveyed exceeds the number employed in a typical screening experiment by 10-20 times. This large number, although impractical for use with actual PCR products, was used to reduce the sampling variation inherent in using a small number of restriction enzymes to assay restriction site differences. Types I and II differed from each other at 36% of the restriction sites found in one or both types. The corresponding frequency of within-type restriction-site differences was 2%. We conclude that the rare within-type restriction-site polymorphisms have a greater than 80% chance of going undetected in routine laboratory surveys employing 10 different restriction enzymes, whereas the more abundant between-type polymorphisms have a less than 1% chance of going undetected under similar conditions. Therefore, if both species had been present in a collection of *C. deitersi* analyzed using only RFLP techniques, the apparent genetic diversity within a "single" taxon would very likely have been inflated.

Our research suggests that type I and type II *C. deitersi* from two locations have similar tolerances to poly-cyclic aromatic hydrocarbons but different tolerances to heavy metals. The results of 96-h bioassays reveal that both type I and type II are very resistant to phenanthrene. Mortality in control populations did not differ from those exposed to concentrations of phenanthrene at the limit of solubility in aqueous solution. *C. deitersi* from Louisiana appears to be more tolerant than other estuarine species. Phenanthrene causes mortality at sediment concentrations below saturation in other benthic harpacticoids (Lotufo and Fleeger, 1997; Lotufo, 1997), and Carman *et al.* (1995; 1997) found that *C. deitersi* survives diesel contamination when most other harpacticoids suffer severe mortality. Type I and type II *C. deitersi* are also both relatively tolerant to a mix of Zn, Pb and Cd (at 6249 μg Zn/l, 685 μg Pb/l and 62 μg Cd/l, based on ratios present in produced water). Mortality in exposed groups was significantly greater than in controls for both species although mortalities were not high enough to calculate an LT_{50} value. However, significant differences between type I and type II were identified; type I (from Alabama) was found to be more tolerant than type II (from Louisiana). Metal resistance often varies with exposure history within species (Klerks and Levinton, 1989b), but inter-specific differences may be associated with the ability to sequester metals (Wallace and Lopez, 1997). Our data suggest that type I and type II would be impacted differently if exposed to metals and that there can be a metal exposure regime in which type II is eliminated from a contaminated site while type II survives.

The large observed genetic differentiation among the lineages of *C. deitersi* suggests long times since initial divergence. Assuming that the rate of molecular evolution in the COX-I gene calibrated in other crustaceans can be applied to *C. deitersi*, copepods from the Salton Sea and Mazatlán appear to have shared a common ancestor between the late Miocene and early Pliocene. The molecular ancestor of lineages II and III dates back to the early and middle Miocene and the oldest divergence between lineages I and II and lineage III to a time between the late Eocene and early Miocene (Table 2.5). These dates are in close agreement with the fossil record. Fossilized specimens assignable to *Cletocamptus* have been found in sedimentary deposits dating to the middle and late Miocene (Palmer 1960). The fossils are similar to an extant species, *C. albuquerquensis* (Herrick), but identifications cannot be confirmed due to a lack of preservation of key characters. However, close resemblance between the fossil and recent *Cletocamptus* suggests a morphological conservatism that has lasted for more than ten million years, a time-scale comparable to the one suggested by molecular data on cryptic species of *C. deitersi*. This long time of divergence, particularly if much of the time since divergence of lineages was spent in contrasting environments, could facilitate the development of differences in tolerances between morphologically-cryptic species. Furthermore, we do not know how common this kind of morphological stasis is among harpacticoids or other meiofaunal taxa. If it is common, the frequency of cryptic species may be higher in meiofauna than in other groups such as small macrofauna. Although it seems unlikely that true cryptic harpacticoids species exist, it is possible that many collections will contain close relatives that are difficult if not impossible to separate without dissection. Gee (1988) found closely-related harpacticoids in sympatry in the Celtic Sea, however no systematic survey has been conducted to determine how often close

14

relatives co-occur in marine habitats. Furthermore, close relatives of common species may be rare within a collection further decreasing the likelihood of detection. Investigators employing harpacticoids for genetic analysis in the future may wish to consider taking the extra precaution of dissecting and archiving a single swimming leg (as was done in this study) to allow limited morphological comparisons among individuals used in genetic analysis. In addition, DNA sequence data offer many advantages over RFLP, and sequencing is replacing RFLP as the mainstay of genetic studies as sequencing cost decreases and the availability of instrumentation increases. Sequence data facilitate the identification of cryptic species or mis-identified individuals by examining all of the nucleotide diversity of the amplified gene regions.

Our research suggests that cryptic species may contribute to the losses of genetic diversity at contaminated sites. This potential reduction occurs by a loss of species at contaminated sites, and a reduction in species diversity is a generally acknowledged consequence of contamination in benthic communities (Peterson et al., 1996). A loss of genetic diversity associated with a reduction in species diversity at contaminated sites is fundamentally different than adaptation-related changes in genetic diversity within species and has an ecological rather than an evolutionary basis. If genetic diversity is used as a marker for contamination effects in the future, the possible contributions of cryptic species should be considered.

3. References

Battaglia, B. 1982. Genetic variation and speciation events in marine copepods. In: *Mechanisms of Speciation* (ed. by C. Bariozzi). New York: A.R. Liss, pp. 377-392.

Bergmans, M. 1979. Taxonomic notes on species of *Tisbe* (Copepoda: Harpacticoida) from a Belgian sluice dock. Zool Scr 8:211-220.

Brown, B.A. 1976. Observations on the tolerance of the isopod *Asellus meridianus* Rac. to copper and lead. Wat Res 10:555-559.

Carman K. R., J. W. Fleeger and S. Pomarico. 1997. Response of a benthic food web to hydrocarbon contamination. Limnol. Oceanogr. 42: 561-571.

Carman K. R., J. W. Fleeger, J. C. Means, S. Pomarico and D. J. McMillin. 1995. Experimental investigation of the effects of polynuclear aromatic hydrocarbons on an estuarine sediment food web. Mar. Environ. Res. 40: 289-318.

Costello, M.J., Emblow, C.S. and Picton, B.E. 1996. Long-term trends in the discovery of marine species new to science which occur in Britain and Ireland. J Mar Biol Assoc UK 76:255-257.

Cunningham, C. W., N. W. Blackstone, and L. W. Buss. 1992. Evolution of king crabs from hermit crab ancestors. Nature 355: 539-542.

DeGiorgi, C., F. DeLuca, C. Stefanile, G. Pesole, and C. Saccone. 1990. Direct evidence that restriction endonucleases may under estimate the degree of divergence between molecules. Curr. Genet. 18:167-168.

DeLaune R. D., C. J. Smith, W. H. Jr. Patrick, J. W. Fleeger and M. D. Tolley. 1984. Effect of oil on salt marsh biota: Methods for restoration. Env. Poll. 36: 207-227.

Dexter D. M. 1995. Salinity tolerance of Cletocamptus deitersi (Richard 1897) and its presence in the Salton Sea. Bull. South. Calif. Acad. Sci 94: 169-171.

Fleeger, J. W. 1980. Morphological variation in *Cletocamptus* (Copepoda: Harpacticoida), with description of a new species from Louisiana salt marshes. Trans. Am. Micro. Soc. 99: 25-31.

Folmer, O., Black, M., Hoeh, W., Lutz, R and Vrijenhoek, R. 1994. DNA primers for amplification of mitochondrial cytochrome c oxidase subunit I from diverse metazoan invertebrates. Mol Mar Biol Biotech 3:294-299.

Ganz, H.H. and Burton, R.S. 1995. Genetic differentiation and reproductive incompatibility among Baja California populations of the copepod *Tigriopus californicus*. Mar Biol 123:821-827.

Gee J. M. 1988. Some harpacticoid copepods (Crustacea) of the family Tachidiidae from sublittoral soft sediments in Norway, the Celtic Sea and Gulf of Mexico. Zool. Scr. 17: 181-194.

Gillespie, R.B. and S.I. Guttman. 1993. Allozyme frequency analysis of aquatic populations as an indicator of contaminant-induced impacts. In *Enviromental Toxicology and Risk Assessment: Vol 2* ASTM STP 1216. J.W. Gorsuch, F.J. Dwyer, C.G. Ingersoll, and T.W. La Point, editors. American Society for Testing and Materials, Philadelphia. 134-145.

Grassle, J.P. and J.F. Grassle. 1976. Sibling species in the marine pollution indicator *Capitella* (Polychaeta). Science 192:567-569.

Heath, D. D., P. D. Rawson, and T. J. Hilbish. 1995. PCR-based nuclear markers identify alien blue mussel (*Mytilus* spp.) genotypes on the west coast of Canada. Can. J. Fish. Aquat. Sci. 52: 2621-2627.

Hebert, P.D.N. and M.M. Luiker. 1996. Genetic effects of contaminant exposure -- towards an assessment of impacts on animal populations. Sci. Total Env. 191:23-58.

Hogg I. D., C. Larose, Y. deLafontaine and K. G. Doe. 1998. Genetic evidence for a *Hyalella* species complex within the Great Lakes St Lawrence River drainage basin: implications for ecotoxicology and conservation biology. Can. J. Zool. 76: 1134-1140.

Hummel, H. and T. Patarnello. 1994. Genetic effects of pollutants on marine and estuarine invertebrates. In *Genetics and Evolution of Aquatic Organisms*. A.R. Beaumont, editor. Chapman and Hall, London. 425-434.

Huys, R., J.M. Gee, C.G.Moore and R. Hamond. 1996. *Marine and brackish water harpacticoid copepods. Part 1.* p. 1-352.

Jukes, T. H. and C. R. Cantor. 1969. Evolution of protein molecules. Pp. 21-132 in H. N. Munro, editor, *Mammalian Protein Metabolism*. Academic Press, New York.

Kennicutt M. C., R. H. Green, P. Montagna and P. F. Roscigno. 1996. Gulf of Mexico offshore operations monitoring experiment (GOOMEX), phase I: Sublethal responses to contaminant exposure - Introduction and overview. Can. J. Fisheries. Aquat. Sci. 53: 2540-2553.

Kimura, M. 1981. Estimation of evolutionary distances between homologous nucleotide sequences. Proc. Natl. Acad. Sci. U. S. A. 78: 454-458.

Klerks, P.L. 1990. Adaptation to metals in animals. In *Heavy metal tolerance in plants: evolutionary aspects*. A.J. Shaw, editor. CRC Press, Boca Raton, FL. 313-321.

Klerks, P.L. and J.S. Levinton. 1989a. Effects of heavy metals in a polluted aquatic ecosystem. In *Ecotoxicology: Problems and approaches*. S.A. Levin, M.A. Harwell, J.R. Kelly, and K.D. Kimball, editors. Springer-Verlag, New York. 41-67.

Klerks, P.L. and J.S. Levinton. 1989b. Rapid evolution of metal resistance in a benthic oligochaete inhabiting a metal-polluted site. Biol. Bull. 176:135-141.

Klerks, P.L. and J.S. Weis. 1987. Genetic adaptation to heavy metals in aquatic organisms: a review. Env. Poll. 45:173-205.

Knowlton, N. 1993. Sibling species in the sea. Ann. Rev. Ecol. Syst. 24: 189-216.

Knowlton, N. and L. A. Weigt. 1998. New dates and new rates for divergence across the Isthmus of Panama. Proc. R. Soc. Lond. Ser. B-Biol. Sci. 265: 2257-2263.

Knowlton, N., L. A. Weigt, L. A. Solorzano, D. K. Mills, and E. Bermingham. 1993. Divergence in proteins, mitochondrial DNA, and reproductive compatibility across the Isthmus of Panama. Science 260: 1629-1632.

Kovatch C. E., N. V. Schizas, G. T. Chandler, B. C. Coull and J. M. Quattro. 2000. Tolerance and genetic relatedness of three meiobenthic copepod populations exposed to sediment-associated contaminant mixtures: role of environmental history. Environ. Toxicol. Chem. 19: 912-919.

Lee W. and R. Huys. 1999. New Normanellidae (Copepoda: Harpacticoida) from western Pacific cold seeps including a review of the genus *Normanella*. Cah. Biol. Mar 40: 203-262.

Linke-Gamenick I., V. E. Forbes and N. Mendez. 2000. Effects of chronic fluoranthene exposure on sibling species of *Capitella* with different development modes. Mar Ecol Prog. Ser. 203:191-203: 191-203.

Lobel, P.B., Belkhode, S.P., Jackson, S.E. and Longerich, H.P. 1990. Recent taxonomic discoveries concerning the mussel *Mytilus*: Implications for biomonitoring. Arch Env Contam Tox 19:508-512.

Lotufo G. R. 1997. Toxicity of sediment-associated PAHs to an estuarine copepod: effects on survival, feeding, reproduction and behavior. Mar. Environ. Res. 44: 149-166.

Lotufo G. R. and J. W. Fleeger. 1997. Effects of sediment-associated phenanthrene on survival, development and reproduction of two species of meiobenthic copepods. Mar. Ecol. Prog. Ser. 151: 91-102.

Mielke, W. 2000. Two new species of *Cletocamptus* (Copepoda : Harpacticoida) from Galapagos, closely related to the cosmopolitan *C. deitersi*. J. Crust. Biol. 20: 273-284.

Mulvey, M. and S.A. Diamond. 1991. Genetic factors and tolerance acquisition in populations exposed to metals and metalloids. In *Metal ecotoxicology: concepts and applications.* M.C. Newman and A.W. McIntosh, editors. Lewis Publishers, Chelsea, MI. 301-321.

Palmer, A. R. 1960. Miocene copepods from the Mojave desert, California. J. Paleontol. 34: 447-452.

Palumbi, S. R. 1996. Nucleic acids II: The polymerase chain reaction. Pp. 205-247 in D. M. Hillis, C. Moritz, and B. K. Mable, editors. Molecular systematics. Sinauer Associates, Inc., Sunderland, Massachusetts.

Pearson, T.H. and R. Rosenberg. 1978. Macrobenthic succession in relation to organic enrichment and pollution of the marine environment. Ocean. Mar. Biol. Ann. Rev. 16:229-311.

Peterson C. H., M. C. Kennicutt, R. H. Green, P. Montagna, D. E. Harper, E. N. Powell and P. F. Roscigno. 1996. Ecological consequences of environmental perturbations associated with offshore hydrocarbon production: A perspective on long-term exposures in the Gulf of Mexico. Can. J. Fish. Aquat. Sci. 53: 2637-2654.

Posada, D. and K. A. Crandall. 1998. MODELTEST: testing the model of DNA substitution. Bioinformatics 14: 817-818.

Posthuma, L. and N.M. VanStraalen. 1993. Heavy metal adaptation in terrestrial invertebrates: a review of occurrence, genetics, physiology and ecological consequences. Comp. Biochem. Physiol. 106C:11-38.

Rambaut, A. and N. C. Grassly. 1997. Seq-Gen: an application for the Monte Carlo simulation of DNA sequence evolution along phylogenetic trees. Comput. Appl. Biosci. 13: 235-238.

Rocha-Olivares, A. 1998. Multiplex haplotype-specific PCR: a new approach for species identification of the early life stages of rockfishes of the species-rich genus *Sebastes* Cuvier. J. Exp. Mar. Biol. Ecol. 231: 279-290.

Rocha-Olivares A., J. W. Fleeger and D. W. Foltz. 2001. Decoupling of molecular and morphological evolution in deep lineages of a meiobenthic harpacticoid copepod. Mol. Biol. Evol. In press:

Rodriguez, F., J. F. Oliver, A. Marin, and J. R. Medina. 1990. The general stochastic model of nucleotide substitution. J. Theor. Biol. 142: 485-501.

Schubart, C. D., R. Diesel, and S. B. Hedges. 1998. Rapid evolution to terrestrial life in Jamaican crabs. Nature 393: 363-365.

Schizas, N. V., G. T. Street, B. C. Coull, G. T. Chandler, and J. M. Quattro. 1997. An efficient DNA extraction method for small metazoans. Mol. Mar. Biol. Biotech. 6: 381-383.

Simpson E. P., M. R. Gonzales, C. M. Hart and S. H. Hurlbert. 1998. Salinity and fish effects on Salton Sea microecosystems: benthos. Hydrobiologia 381: 153-177.

Street G. T. and P. A. Montagna. 1996. Loss of genetic diversity in Harpacticoida near offshore platforms. Mar. Biol. 126: 271-282.

Street G. T., G. R. Lotufo, P. A. Montagna and J. W. Fleeger. 1998. Reduced genetic diversity in a meiobenthic copepod exposed to a xenobiotic. J. Exp. Mar. Biol. Ecol. 222: 93-111.

Sturmbauer, C., J. S. Levinton, and J. Christy. 1996. Molecular phylogeny analysis of fiddler crabs: Test of the hypothesis of increasing behavioral complexity in evolution. Proc. Natl. Acad. Sci. 93: 10855-10857.

Sturmbauer C., G. B. Opadiya, H. Niederstatter, A. Riedmann and R. Dallinger. 1999. Mitochondrial DNA reveals cryptic oligochaete species differing in cadmium resistance. Mol. Biol. Evol. 16: 967-974.

Sun, B. and J. W. Fleeger. 1994. Field experiments on the colonization of meiofauna into sediment depressions. Mar. Ecol.-Prog. Ser. 110: 167-175.

Swofford, D. L. 1998. *PAUP*: Phylogenetic Analysis Using Parsimony (* and other methods). Version 4.0*, Sinauer, Sunderland, Massachusetts.

Thompson, J. D., D. G. Higgins, and T. J. Gibson. 1994. CLUSTAL W: Improving the sensitivity of progressive multiple sequence alignment through sequence weighting, position-specific gap penalties and weight matrix choice. Nuc. Acids Res. 22: 4673-4680.

Todaro, M.A., Fleeger, J.W., Hu, Y.P., Hrincevich, A.W. and Foltz, D.W. 1996. Are meiofaunal species cosmopolitan? Morphological and molecular analysis of *Xenotrichula intermedia* (Gastrotricha: Chaetonotida). Mar Biol. 125: 735-742.

Wallace W. G. and G. R. Lopez. 1997. Bioavailability of biologically sequestered cadmium and the implications of metal detoxification. Mar. Ecol. Progr. Ser. 147: 149-157.

Warwick, R.M. and Clarke, K.R. 1995. New 'biodiversity' measures reveal a decrease in taxonomic distinctness with increasing stress. Mar Ecol Prog Ser 129:301-305.

Yang, Z. H. 1997. PAML: a program package for phylogenetic analysis by maximum likelihood. Comput. Appl. Biosci. 13: 555-556.

Yang, Z. and R. Nielsen. 1998. Synonymous and nonsynonymous rate variation in nuclear genes of mammals. J. Mol. Evol. 46: 409-418.

Yang, Z. 1993. Maximum-likelihood estimation of phylogeny from DNA sequences when substitution rates differ over sites. Mol. Biol. Evol. 10: 1396-1401.

MHS-PCR

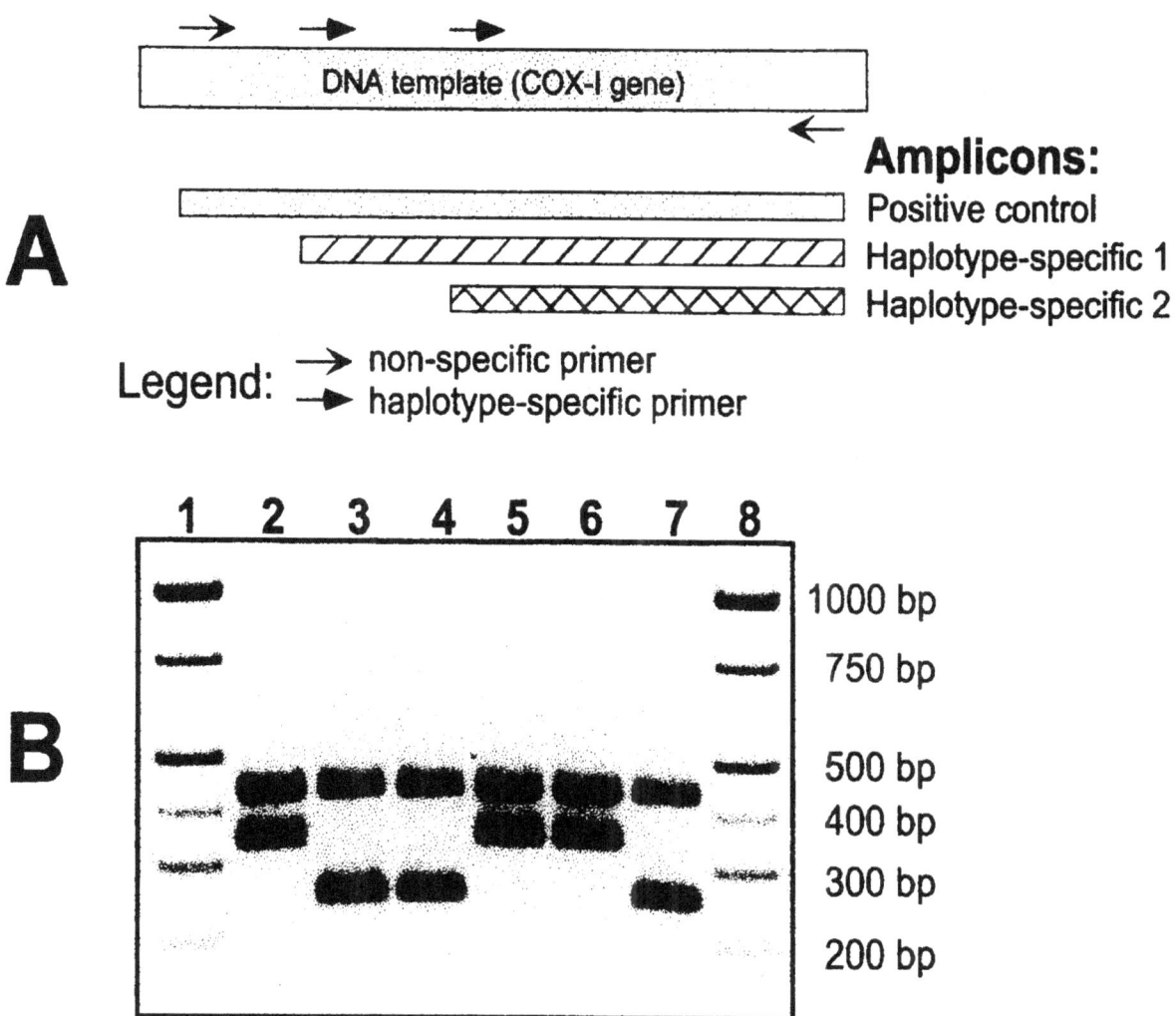

Figure 2.1 Multiple haplotype-specific PCR (MHS-PCR) used to genotype individual *Cletocamptus deitersi* based on COX-I amplification. A) A pair of non-specific primers is used as positive control and an additional pair of haplotype-specific primers yields amplicons of diagnostic size used for genotyping. B) Negative gel image of the results obtained with *C. deitersi*. Lanes 1 and 8 are molecular markers; lane 2 is a type I copepod verified by direct sequencing (427 and 349 bp bands); lanes 3 and 4 are unknown copepods from Louisiana; lanes 5 and 6 are unknown copepods from Alabama; and lane 7 is a type II copepod verified by direct sequencing (427 and 253 bp bands).

23

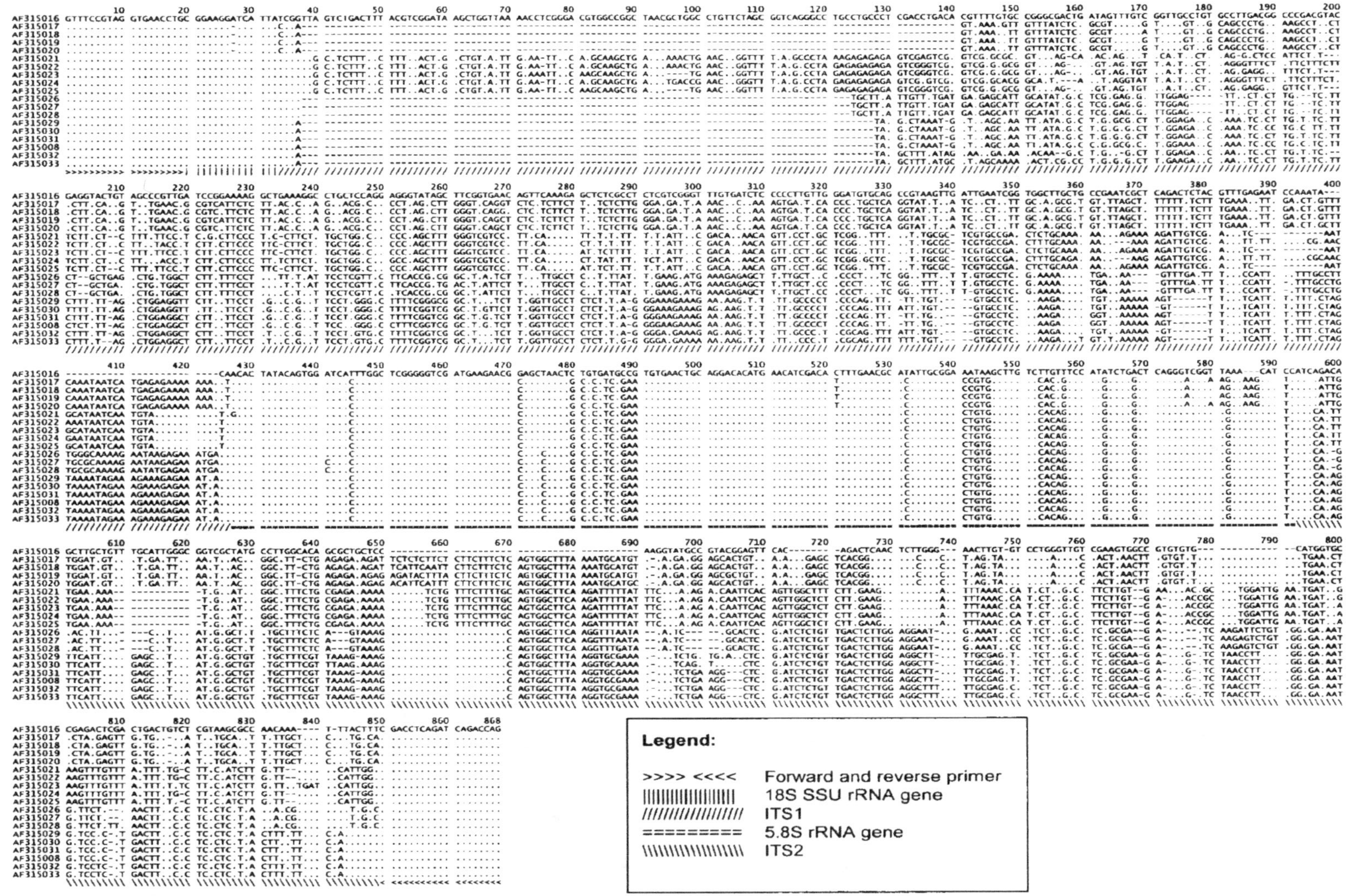

Figure 2.2 Clustal W DNA multiple alignment of part of the nuclear rDNA comprising the entire internal transcribed spacers (ITS1 and ITS2) and the intervening 5.8S ribosomal RNA gene. Gene regions are indicated at the bottom of the alignment. Labels refer to Genbank accession numbers presented in Table 2.1. Dots represent identity with the majority rule consensus sequence on top and dashes represent inferred indels.

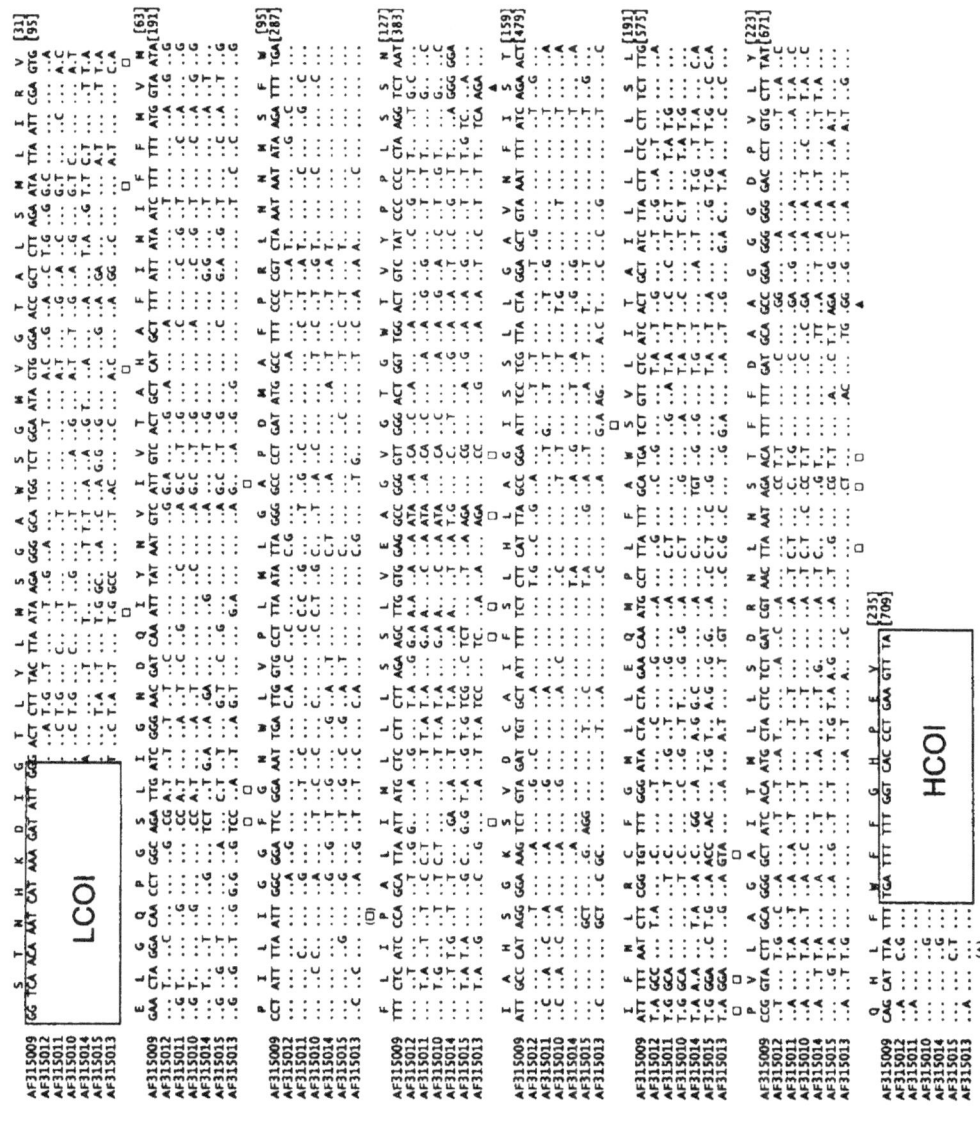

Figure 2.3 DNA multiple alignment of representative sequences of the mitochondrial cytochrome oxidase I gene bounded by Folmer *et al.* (1994) LCOI and HCOI primers. A translation of the reading frame is provided for the first reference sequence, dots indicate identity with it. Symbols below the nucleotides refer to conservative (□) and non-conservative (▲) amino acid substitutions. Symbols in parentheses indicate that the amino acid substitution was found in a sequence not included in the alignment

25

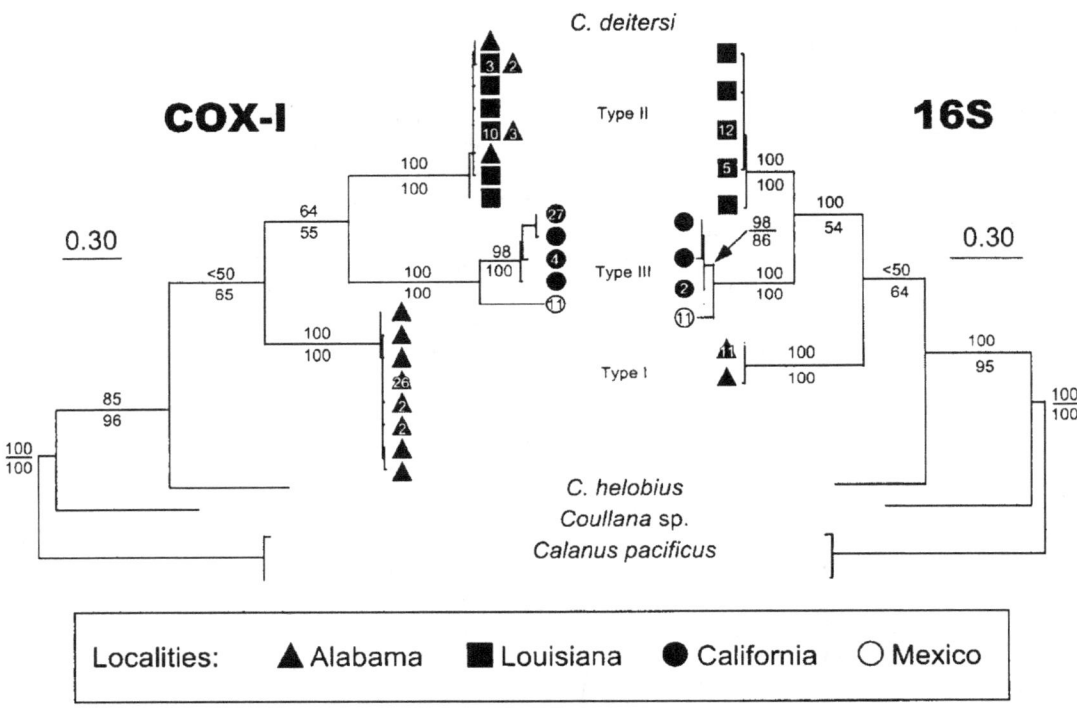

Figure 2.4 Neighbor-Joining (NJ) phylogenetic reconstructions based on genetic distances of distinct mitochondrial cytochrome oxidase subunit I (COX-I, K81uf+I+G distances) and 16S ribosomal RNA (16S, TIM+I+G distances) haplotypes of the harpacticoid copepods *Cletocamptus deitersi*, *C. helobius*, *Coullana* sp., and the calanoid copepod *Calanus pacificus*. Branch lengths are proportional to genetic distance according to scales shown. Numbers on branches are non-parametric bootstrap support values (1000 replications) obtained with NJ (above) and with maximum parsimony (below). Localities where haplotypes were found are indicated by symbols, numbers in symbols are the number of copepods sharing a particular haplotype.

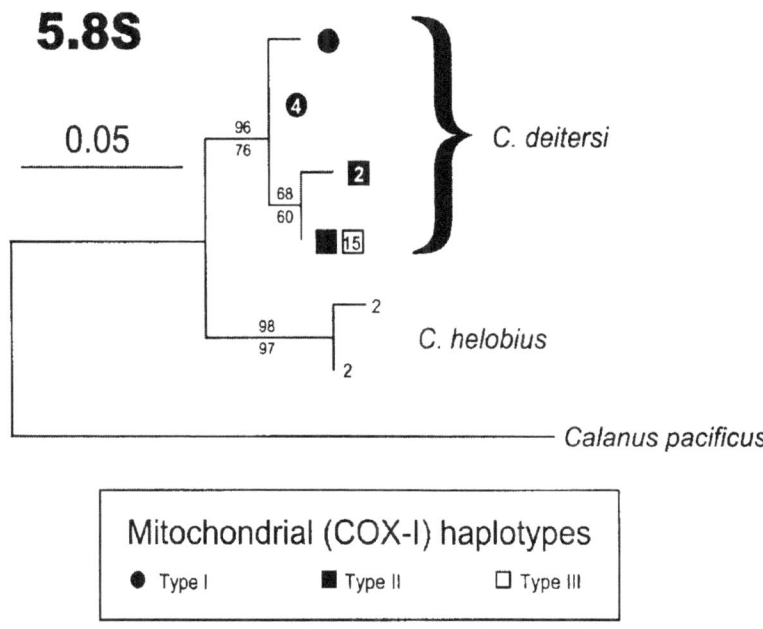

Figure 2.5 Neighbor-Joining (NJ) phylogenetic reconstruction based on Jukes-Cantor genetic distances of distinct nuclear 5.8S ribosomal RNA alleles of the harpacticoid copepods *Cletocamptus deitersi*, *C. helobius*, and the calanoid copepod *Calanus pacificus*. Branch lengths represent genetic distances according to the scale shown. Numbers on branches represent nonparametric bootstrap support values (1000 replicates) obtained with NJ (above) and with maximum parsimony (below). The corresponding mitochondrial haplotype found in the same copepods is indicated by the symbols. Numbers in symbols represent the individuals sharing the same 5.8S rRNA gene copy.

27

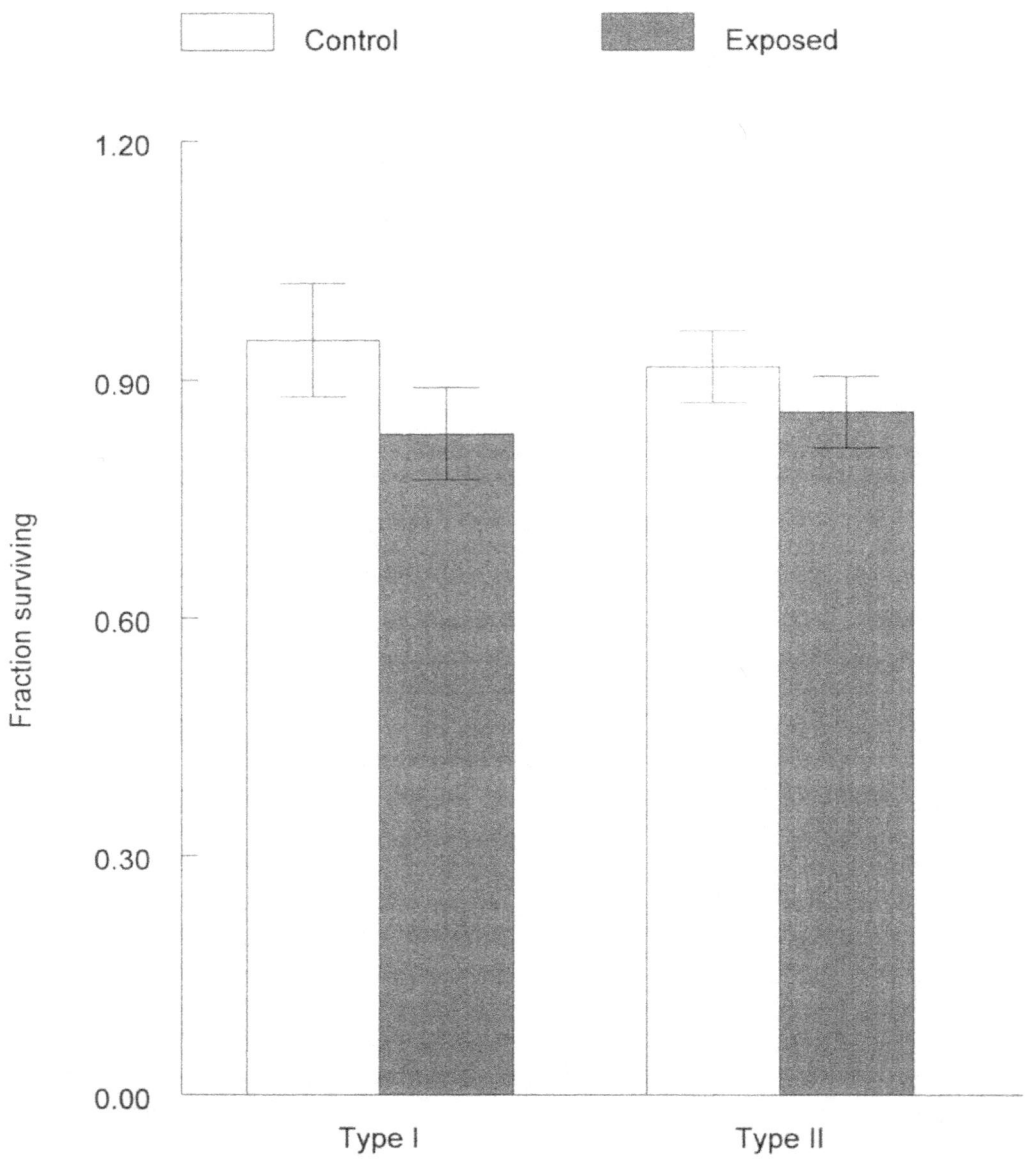

Figure 2.6. Percent survival of type I and II *Cletocamptus deitersi* for individuals exposed and unexposed (control) to saturated phenanthrene for 96 hours. Error bars show ± one standard deviation. There was no variation among replicates for the type II control individuals.

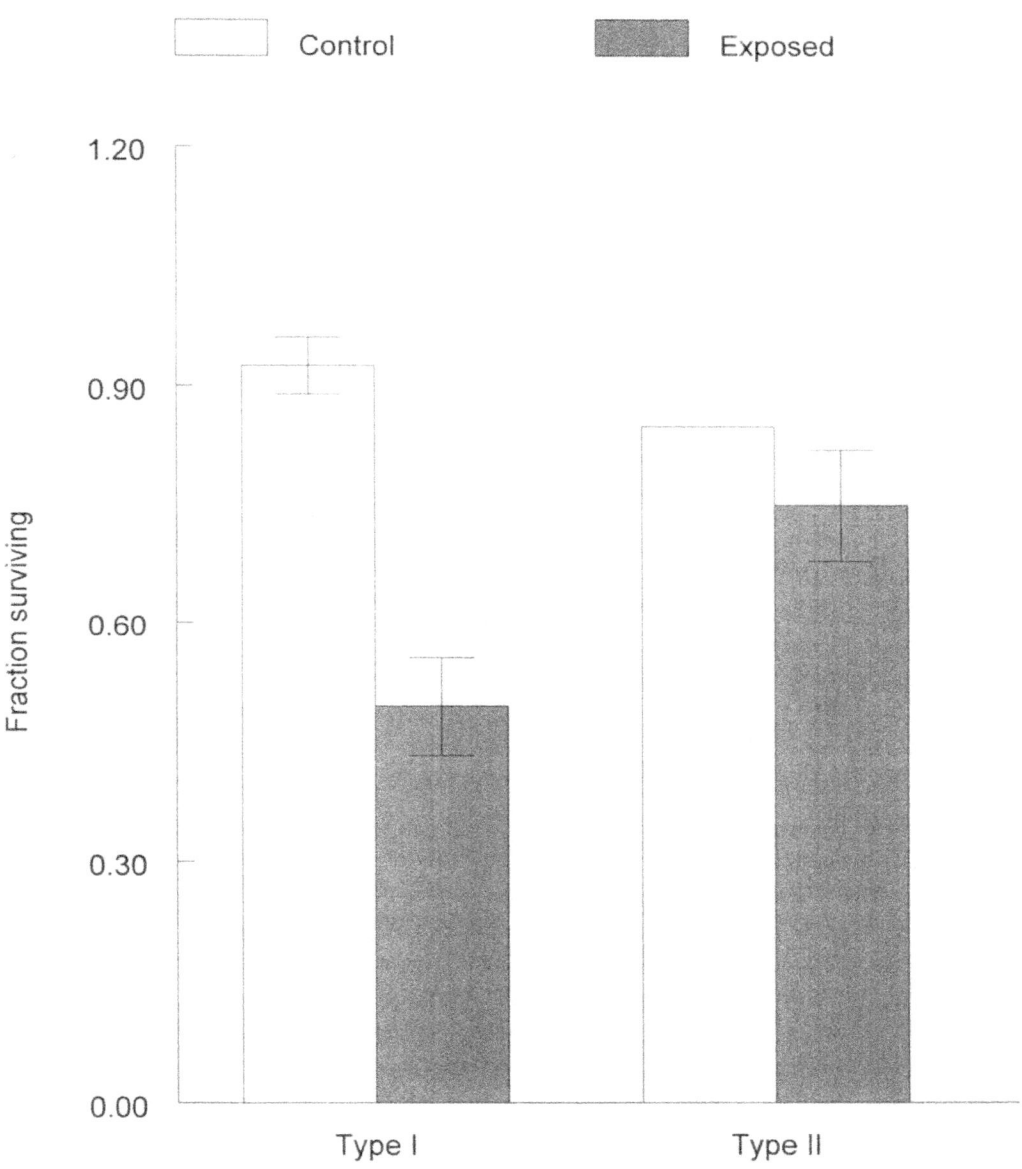

Figure 2.7 Percent survival of type I and II *Cletocamptus deitersi* for individuals exposed and unexposed (control) to a mix of heavy metals (see text for composition) for 96 hours. Error bars show ± one standard deviation.

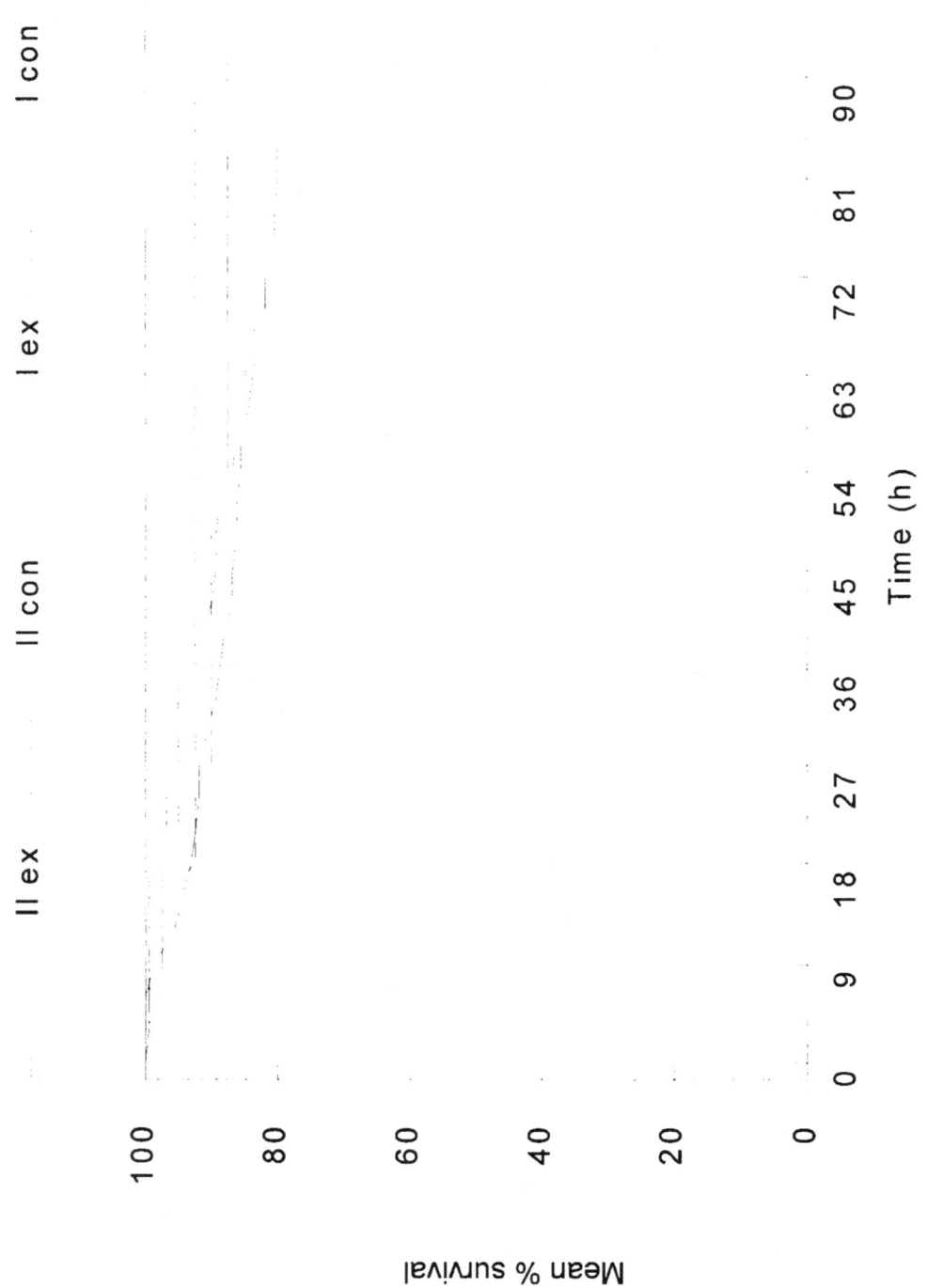

Figure 2.8 Survivorship curves of type I and II *Cletocamptus deitersi* in 96-hour exposures to heavy metals. I ex = type I exposed to metals, I con = type I not exposed, II ex = type II exposed to metals and II con = type II not exposed to metals.

Table 2.1.

Number of copepods (n), number of distinct mtDNA haplotypes or nuclear gene copies (h), and accession numbers of representative sequences submitted to Genbank (GB), of each copepod species genotyped by direct sequencing (COX-I, 16S, n rDNA) or multiplex haplotype-specific PCR of the COX-I gene (MHS).

Species (sample)	COX-I[a]			16S[b]			n rDNA[c]			MHS
	n	h	GB	n	h	GB	n	h[d]	GB	n
Cletocamptus deitersi (AL)[e]	42	10	AF315009	12	2	AF315001	5	5/2/5	AF315021-25	55
Cletocamptus deitersi (LA)	17	6	AF315012	20	5	AF315002	3	3/2/3	AF315026-28	126
Cletocamptus deitersi (CA)	33	4	AF315011	4	3	AF315003	4	4/1/4	AF315008+29-31	0
Cletocamptus deitersi (MX)	11	1	AF315010	11	1	AF315004	11	2/1/1	AF315033-34	0
Cletocamptus helobius	6	1	AF315014	3	1	AF315005	4	4/2/4	AF315017-20	0
Coullana sp.	2	1	AF315015	1	1	AF315007	0	--	---	0
Calanus pacificus	3	3	AF315013	4	3	AF315006	1	1	AF315016	0

[a] mitochondrial cytochrome oxidase subunit I
[b] mitochondrial LSU rDNA (16S)
[c] nuclear rDNA consisting of ITS1, 5.8S rRNA gene, and ITS2
[d] number of distinct ITS1/5.8S rRNA/ITS2 gene copies
[e] AL= Alabama, LA= Louisiana, CA= California, MX= Mazatlán, Mexico

Table 2.2

Mean pairwise genetic distances in the COX-I (above diagonal) and 16S (below diagonal)[a] mitochondrial genes in four lineages of *Cletocamptus deitersi* (types I, II, IIIC, and IIIM) and in *C. helobius* (CH).

	Type I	Type II	Type IIIC	Type IIIM	CH
Type I	[b]0.27 (0.2-0.5) n=28 0.35 n=1 n=1	23.15 (22.5-25.3) 61.59 (58.5-74.4) [c] n=64	24.68 (24.0-26.1) 68.44 (62.2-82.0) n=32	26.27 (26.1-26.4) 76.70 (73.9-88.3) n=8	26.77 (24.5-26.8) 79.67 (77.3-91.7) n=8
Type II	32.15 (31.4-32.4) 58.03 (56.0-58.9) n=10	0.33 (0.2-0.6) n=28 0.69 (0.3-1.0) n=10	21.49 (20.8-22.0) 51.28 (48.7-53.4) n=32	22.13 (22.0-22.3) 52.02 (51.2-53.0) n=8	23.82 (23.7-24.0) 72.80 (71.9-74.1) n=8
Type IIIC	35.77 (35.6-36.0) 80.76 (79.1-82.5) n=6	20.92 (20.3-21.3) 30.54 (29.4-31.2) n=15	1.19 (0.2-1.7) n=6 0.69 (0.3-1.0) n=3	8.66 (8.4-8.8) 11.04 (10.6-11.3) n=4	26.37 (26.1-26.6) 88.45 (80.5-82.0) n=4
Type IIIM	35.68 (35.7-35-7) 82.16 (81.8-82.5) n=2	21.07 (20.7-21.1) 31.67 (30.9-32.2) n=5	4.48 (4.1-4.8) 4.64 (4.3-5.0) n=3	[d] n.a.	25.84 79.26 n=1
CH	35.77 (35.8-35.8) 81.12 (80.8-81.4) n=2	31.96 (31.7-32.1) 63.57 (63.1-63.9) n=5	32.89 (32.6-33.0) 70.17 (69.9-70.5) n=3	32.28 68.51 n=1	n.a.

[a] 16S distances computed on 16SAR-16SBR fragment corrected for missing data for type IIIM and CH
[b] In diagonal. line 1 = COX-I, line 2 = 16S (mean uncorrected %p, n=*number of comparisons*)
[c] Off diagonal. line 1 = uncorrected %p, line 2 = %K81uf+I+G (COX-I) and %TIM+I+G (16S) (range in parentheses),
     Line 3   n = *number of comparisons.*
[d] Not applicable

Table 2.3

Mean uncorrected genetic distances (%) in the ITS1, 5.8S, and ITS2 genes regions in four lineages of *Cletocamptus deitersi* (types I, II, IIIC, and IIIM) and in *C. helobius* (CH).

Gene	Comparison	Mean	n^a	Range
ITS-1	type I x type I	7.63	10	0.6-12.6
	type II x type II	2.73	3	2.1-3.4
	type IIIC x type IIIC	4.06	6	2.4-5.9
	type IIIM x type IIIM	8.50	1	n.a.[b]
	type IIIC x type IIIM	11.95	8	8.5-15.7
ITS-2	type I x type I	0.73	10	0.0-1.4
	type II x type II	0.65	3	0.5-1.0
	type IIIC x type IIIC	2.60	3	1.8-3.2
	type IIIM x type IIIM	n.a.	0	n.a.
	type IIIC x type IIIM	2.80	3	1.4-4.6
5.8S [c]	type I x type I	0.61	1	n.a.
	type II x type II	0.61	1	n.a.
	type III x type III	n.a.	0	n.a.
	type I x type II	1.53	2	1.2-1.8
	type I x type III	0.92	2	0.6-1.2
	type II x type III	0.61	1	n.a.
	CH x type I	3.70	4	3.1-4.3
	CH x type II	4.62	2	4.3-4.9
	CH x type III	3.99	2	3.7-4.3

[a] Number of pair-wise comparisons averaged

[b] Not applicable

[c] All type III copepods from California (IIIC) and Mazatlán (IIIM) shared the same 5.8S gene copy.

33

Table 2.4

Parameters of the models of nucleotide substitution fit to mitochondrial and nuclear genes of *C. deitersi*.

Gene	Model[a]	Base frequencies (ACG)	Rate matrix[b]	I[c]	G[d]
COX-I	Kimura 81	0.2689, 0.1688, 0.2051	r(A_G) = 9.778 r(A_T) = 2.014	0.435	1.141
16S rDNA	TIM	0.4024, 0.1518, 0.1443	r(A_G) = 8.327 r(A_T) = 3.047 r(C_T) = 11.053	0.222	4.235
5.8S rDNA	JC	0.25, 0.25, 0.25	r(N_notN) = 1.0	n.a.[e]	n.a.

[a] Kimura 81 (Kimura 1981), TIM (Rodriguez *et al.* 1990), and JC (Jukes and Cantor 1969)
[b] relative rates to r(A_C) fixed at 1.0, only distinct elements of the matrix are shown
[c] proportion of invariable sites
[d] shape parameter of the Gamma distribution assumed to describe rate heterogeneity among sites
[e] not applicable

Table 2.5

Ranges of divergence since common ancestor based on corrected sequence divergence and crustacean molecular clock calibrations [a].

	16S		COX-I	
Common ancestor of	Mean corrected distance (%)[b]	Divergence range (Ma)[b]	Mean corrected distance (%)[b]	Divergence range (Ma)[b]
IIIM and IIIC	4.66K	5.1K - 12.3K	9.35K - 11.11H	3.9K - 7.9H
II and III	24.52K	27.2K - 64.5K	26.20K - 40.67H	10.9K - 29.1H
I and II, III	46.83K	52.0K - 123.2K	30.56K - 51.17H	12.7K - 36.6H

[a] Rates of molecular evolution used for the 16S rRNA gene include 0.38% Kimura 2-parameter/Ma for anomurans (Cunningham *et al.* 1992) and 0.90% Kimura 2-parameter/Ma for fiddler crabs (Sturmbauer *et al.* 1996). A second calibration of 0.65-0.88% Kimura 2-parameter/Ma (Schubart *et al.* 1998) obtained from grapsid crabs gives intermediate values. COX-I calibrations of geminate species of alpheid shrimps include 1.4% maximum likelihood-Γ/Ma (Knowlton and Weigt 1998) and 2.4% Kimura 2-parameter/Ma (Knowlton *et al.* 1993). A third calibration of 1.66% Kimura 2-parameter/Ma (Schubart *et al.* 1998) obtained from grapsid crabs also gives intermediate values.

[b] Letters after values refer to the correction using the HKY85-Γ (H) or the Kimura 2-parameter model (K). These models were used in order to match those used in the calibrations, best fit models would produce older estimates.

The Department of the Interior Mission

As the Nation's principal conservation agency, the Department of the Interior has responsibility for most of our nationally owned public lands and natural resources. This includes fostering sound use of our land and water resources; protecting our fish, wildlife, and biological diversity; preserving the environmental and cultural values of our national parks and historical places; and providing for the enjoyment of life through outdoor recreation. The Department assesses our energy and mineral resources and works to ensure that their development is in the best interests of all our people by encouraging stewardship and citizen participation in their care. The Department also has a major responsibility for American Indian reservation communities and for people who live in island territories under U.S. administration.

The Minerals Management Service Mission

As a bureau of the Department of the Interior, the Minerals Management Service's (MMS) primary responsibilities are to manage the mineral resources located on the Nation's Outer Continental Shelf (OCS), collect revenue from the Federal OCS and onshore Federal and Indian lands, and distribute those revenues.

Moreover, in working to meet its responsibilities, the **Offshore Minerals Management Program** administers the OCS competitive leasing program and oversees the safe and environmentally sound exploration and production of our Nation's offshore natural gas, oil and other mineral resources. The MMS **Minerals Revenue Management** meets its responsibilities by ensuring the efficient, timely and accurate collection and disbursement of revenue from mineral leasing and production due to Indian tribes and allottees, States and the U.S. Treasury.

The MMS strives to fulfill its responsibilities through the general guiding principles of: (1) being responsive to the public's concerns and interests by maintaining a dialogue with all potentially affected parties and (2) carrying out its programs with an emphasis on working to enhance the quality of life for all Americans by lending MMS assistance and expertise to economic development and environmental protection.

www.ingramcontent.com/pod-product-compliance
Lightning Source LLC
Chambersburg PA
CBHW081125280526
45787CB00007B/2979